LIVING

Living the Lord's Prayer

Archbishop Rowan Williams
and Sister Wendy Beckett

COMPILED BY SU BOX

LION

Copyright © 2005 BBC and Rowan Williams
This edition copyright © 2007 Lion Hudson

The authors assert the moral right
to be identified as the authors of this work

A Lion Book
an imprint of
Lion Hudson plc
Mayfield House, 256 Banbury Road,
Oxford OX2 7DH, England
www.lionhudson.com
ISBN 978 0 7459 5233 8

First edition 2007
10 9 8 7 6 5 4 3 2 1 0

Acknowledgments

By arrangement with the BBC. BBC logo © BBC 1996.
The BBC logo is a registered trademark of the British
Broadcasting Corporation and is used under licence.

A catalogue record for this book is available
from the British Library

Typeset in Venetian301 BT
Printed and bound in China

Contents

Living the Lord's Prayer

Introduction

The Lord's Prayer, also often called the 'Our Father', is the world's most well-known and best-loved Christian prayer. Its words are used by Christians of all denominations (and none) in every continent and it is one of the few prayers that most believers are able to say by heart. Yet how often do we pause to consider the meaning of its familiar phrases?

When BBC Television's *Songs of Praise* programme dedicated an entire edition to the Lord's Prayer, the audience response demonstrated the enduring appeal of this prayer to people today. As well as the usual musical selection that makes *Songs of Praise* so popular, the programme included interviews

with Rowan Williams, the Archbishop of Canterbury, and Sister Wendy Beckett. This book enables us to share some of their insights as they reflect on the significance and meaning of this timeless prayer. In addition, also based on the *Songs of Praise* recording, there are moving personal accounts showing how two men were challenged by particular phrases in the Lord's Prayer and the impact this had on their lives.

The familiar words of the Lord's Prayer can trip off the tongue so easily that we rarely take time to think of the importance of what we are saying. *Living the Lord's Prayer* provides an opportunity to discover how each phrase is packed with meaning if we take time to reflect. It will enrich our understanding of the words Jesus said when his disciples asked him: 'Lord, how should we pray?'

The Lord's Prayer

Our Father, who art in heaven,
hallowed be thy name.

Thy Kingdom come, thy will be done,
on earth as it is in heaven.

Give us this day our daily bread,

And forgive us our trespasses,
as we forgive those who trespass against us.

Lead us not into temptation,
but deliver us from evil.

For thine is the kingdom, the power
and the glory, for ever and ever.

Amen

TRADITIONAL VERSION TAKEN FROM
THE BOOK OF COMMON PRAYER

Living the Lord's Prayer

'Lord, teach us to pray,' was the request of Jesus' disciples. Rather than responding with a lesson, his answer was to give a short, simple and memorable model to follow – the words of the Lord's Prayer. As well as giving us insights into Jesus' own prayer life and teaching, it's a prayer that encompasses all our spiritual and material well-being, and one that can have a transforming effect if we make it part of our everyday lives. Before looking at the prayer in detail, let's consider some of the issues that are often raised about its significance and relevance to our lives today.

A prayer for today?

Some people ask how a prayer that's almost two thousand years old can have any relevance in the twenty-first century. Yet, as we will discover, the Lord's Prayer relates well to the experiences of people today and the issues they may have to contend with. Sister Wendy has no doubt that the value of the Lord's Prayer is timeless:

> *The teaching of Jesus is for all time. As long as human beings are human, we'll need what Jesus taught and what the Our Father sums up. There can never be a time when the Our Father becomes irrelevant.*

Her view is echoed by Rowan Williams, who believes that the Lord's Prayer is today not only relevant but also as radical as it would have been when shared with its first hearers. He says:

> *It's completely fresh, it never gets stale because what it's talking about is the human condition in the presence of God. It's about the world we live in and the world God wants us to live in, and I can't imagine anything taking its place.*
>
> *... Every single bit of the Lord's Prayer is radical because it challenges our assumptions about who we are and who God is and what the world is like. And what it's praying for is the most revolutionary change you can*

imagine in the world we live in. A change to a situation where all the hungry are fed, to a situation where forgiveness is the first imperative, and all our relationships are transparent to God. And, as people will notice, that's not exactly like the world we inhabit at the moment — it's looking for change from the roots up.

Overfamiliarity

Many Christians say the words of the Lord's Prayer time after time, every week or sometimes every day. So isn't there a danger of becoming too familiar with what we are praying for? Sister Wendy, who spends most of her time in prayer and for whom the prayer is a fundamental part of daily life, is certain there is no risk of this:

> '*We can never be too familiar with the Lord's Prayer.*'

I don't think we can ever be too familiar with the Lord's Prayer or that it would be possible to overestimate its importance. After all, this is what Jesus himself said when he was asked 'Lord, teach us how to pray'. It sums up the whole of our faith.

However, it has been said that we know the Lord's Prayer so well that we don't think about the words. How can we get around this age-old problem? Sister Wendy has a solution:

> *I think it's a very good spiritual exercise to take a phrase and work through it, perhaps for several weeks, thinking and praying it. When you say it the words go too quickly, they just slip past. That's all right - but they're really too deep to understand while you say them; understanding is for meditation.*

A pattern for prayer

Jesus often taught using parables – simple memorable stories – and he also wanted his followers to be able to bring the words of this prayer readily to mind. Rowan Williams reminds us of the value of having both words and a pattern for prayer that are easy to remember:

> *Jesus is teaching an easily memorable form of words, an easily memorable form of prayer. So it's meant to be transmitted, it's meant to be learned and taught, and passed on... These are the words that Jesus commends to us and, of course, the prayer gives us a template for*

other sorts of prayer and an inspiration for the nature of all the prayers we ever offer.

Similarly, the idea of using the prayer as a framework around which we can build our own prayers is important to Sister Wendy:

> *Obviously the Lord's Prayer is about attitudes, attitudes of trust and love and forgiveness, and about exposing needs. It doesn't really matter how you express those things, but this is a good shorthand… You don't have to use this formula; Jesus was just telling you this is the kind of attitude you must have, for which I for one am extremely grateful.*
>
> *The Our Father is absolutely part of me and of my daily life. I would hope that the attitudes of the Our Father are slowly but surely becoming part of me. I long for them to be of my essence.*

Our Father, who art in heaven, hallowed be thy name

The sentences of the Lord's Prayer are multilayered and every phrase is packed with meaning for those who want to look deeper. It is certainly the case for this first phrase.

The family prayer

Whether we call it the Lord's Prayer or the Our Father, this prayer is one that unites all Christians. Rowan Williams says:

> *Because the first word of the Lord's Prayer is 'Our' not 'My', you're always saying it, in some sense, with*

other Christians. You're always saying 'This is what I most deeply share with other Christian believers and so even when I'm saying it on my own it's with everybody else.'

... But what's absolutely unique about it is that it begins simply with the address 'Our Father', nothing else. Nothing more elaborate, nothing more grand, but just that address as to the father of the family. This is the prayer of God's family. And this is the prayer which you address to God in the most intimate of terms.

> **'This is the prayer of God's family.'**

Perhaps knowing that we belong to God's family helps give us the confidence to pray? Rowan Williams reminds us:

When we say 'Our Father', we need to remember that it's a bold form of address to God. Yet Jesus has given us the nerve to call God 'Father' - you sometimes hear it introduced as 'the prayer Our Saviour has taught us'.

These opening words are of particular importance to Sister Wendy:

If I were asked to summarize the Lord's Prayer I would take that first phrase, 'Our Father', because that is essentially the message of Jesus: that the great God - that total mystery whom we can't comprehend with our minds - that great mysterious reality is Our Father.

... The wonder of having God as our father was something only Jesus really knew, because he could see. We live in faith, but it's the same father, my father and your father. 'Our Father' extends to all of us... Our Father: we as human beings have a father, a father who couldn't love us more.

Intimacy with God

Most of Jesus' followers would have identified echoes of prayers from the Jewish tradition – in which he was brought up – in the Lord's Prayer. Yet they would have noticed a striking difference in the way Jesus addressed God. Rowan Williams explains:

> *It's quite clear from the New Testament that the one thing people remembered about Jesus' own prayers and about his teaching on prayer was that he called God 'Father'. He used the familiar word 'Abba', the intimate word for 'father' in his own language. So the first thing that Jesus says when he talks to God is 'Father'. He doesn't call God 'Creator' or 'Lord' or 'Master', he says 'Father'. The first word he says affirms his relationship with God.*

Rowan Williams goes on to remind us that by using these two simple words Jesus showed Christians that they too could approach God in a personal way, sharing this intimacy with God:

> *When the words 'Our Father' are said we ought perhaps to think of that resurrection incident where Jesus speaks to a close friend and follower about 'my Father and your Father'. And so as soon as you've said the first words, 'Our Father', you've said, 'I've been*

given a share in Jesus' relationship with God; I don't
have to work out my relationship with God from
scratch; I don't have to climb a long ladder up to
heaven; I've been invited into this family relationship.'
And that's the gift that every prayer begins with.

A heavenly father

It's all too easy for our picture of a heavenly father to
be influenced by our experiences of our earthly fathers
and, for some, these experiences may be unhelpful.
Sister Wendy is particularly concerned for those with a
poor image of fatherhood for whom the opening phrase
of this prayer might be a stumbling block:

> *Our Father* in heaven: *That to me is crucial… So*
> *many people have difficulties in their faith because they*
> *expect God the Father to be like an earthly father. So*
> *when they pray they expect what they would get from an*
> *earthly father, and they're not going to get it.*
>
> *When you hear the word 'Father' or 'Dad' or*
> *'Daddy', that word brings back an enormous amount of*
> *memories and meanings. There are some people who*
> *have difficulty with the Our Father because they have*
> *had an abusive father, so the word 'Father' is hateful to*
> *them. And then, I would imagine, they have to spend a*
> *long time in prayer understanding the difference.*

Sister Wendy goes on to explain that having a 'good' father can present surprising difficulties – until we understand the difference between an earthly father and a heavenly father:

> *The most wonderful earthly father, the kind I had myself, warm and loving, who would do anything for his children, can provide earthly things: food, clothing, education, smiles, kisses, love, praise, all those encouraging, warm, tangible things… Our heavenly father, if we ask him for a need, gives us these things and* much more *but not in an earthly way. To understand*

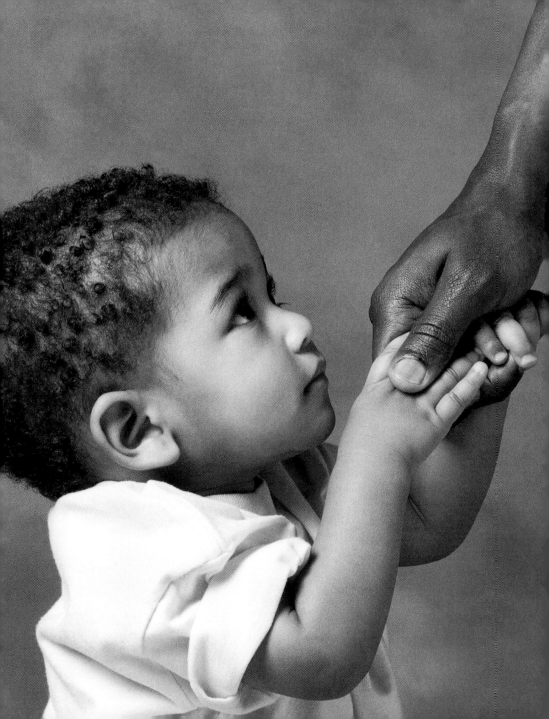

that the prayer is always answered, but in a heavenly way, is very difficult. It needs great faith and great understanding.

An earthly father is visibly there. When he puts his arms around you, his presence is there, comforting you. Not so for the heavenly father. Yet though we may not feel his presence, it simply means he's a father in heaven, not that he doesn't care for us. His is the kind of fatherhood beyond anybody's imagining.

Growing up

Thinking of God as Father doesn't mean that we're always going to have a childlike relationship with him. God wants us to 'grow up' and develop a mature relationship with him. Rowan Williams explains something of what this means for us:

In the context of Jesus' life and of the New Testament, it's not at all about a fatherhood that makes us dependent and childish. To know that God is our Father is to know that nothing can take away our dignity and our worth, because God has thought us worthy to be members of his family. And in the light of that we can take all sorts of risks; we can grow into all kinds of freedom... Being able to take risks, knowing that the Father will always be there to forgive and to give you new beginnings - that's how we grow up. Jesus' own life is the measure of that; he's completely dependent on God, and yet he's as free as anybody could be imagined to be.

Sister Wendy echoes these words and goes on to remind us how this dependency also means that God is ultimately in control:

When we call God 'Father', we accept that this is a relationship, and it's a relationship we will grow through. Well, we'll grow through it if we accept the grace of God to lead us through it... He doesn't want us to be childishly dependent, unable to think for ourselves, but he wants us to be childlike in our dependence, thinking for ourselves, using our conscience, full adults but not in control... We're never in control with God. We're in control in that it's up to us how we respond to him, but we're not in control as to what happens to us.

Our heavenly home

If our Father is in heaven then that, ultimately, is the home of his children. This is something that Christians

can both look forward to and experience to some degree here on earth, as Rowan Williams reminds us:

> *When we say this, we're saying heaven - God's place, God's home - is also our home. As St Paul says in one of his letters, our citizenship is in heaven - that is, heaven is where we belong. And the kind of relationship that exists in God's presence in heaven is a relationship of love and trust and intimacy and praise that can be ours here and now. Such short simple words - and yet they tell us that heaven is here on earth because of Jesus, and we can enter into that.*

'Heaven is where we belong.'

Honouring God's name

The somewhat archaic-sounding phrase 'Hallowed be thy name' is one that doesn't translate easily into contemporary language. Rowan Williams explains that those in the early church would have understood the significance of standing in awe and reverence before God, something that too few people appreciate today. He suggests that it is helpful to remember the context in which this phrase was first spoken:

> *I want to see it against the background of the Old Testament's idea that the name of God is something in itself immensely beautiful and powerful. The name of God is God's word, God's presence. And to ask that*

God's name be hallowed, God's name be looked upon as holy, is to ask that in the world people will understand the presence of God among them with awe and reverence… And that they will approach the name of God, the word of God, with the veneration and humility that's demanded.

'The name of God is something in itself immensely beautiful and powerful.'

He continues with a warning that we're not to trivialize the name of God by using it as a kind of 'magic' talisman, bringing it down to our level to try to make God a tool for our purposes. It should be spoken with awe.

When you say 'Hallowed be thy name', understand what you're talking about - you're talking about God. This is serious; this is the most wonderful and frightening reality that we could imagine. More wonderful and frightening than we can ever imagine. And that's why it's all the more extraordinary that we should be able to approach God as Father.

As well as helping us to approach a holy God with a sense of awe, the words 'Hallowed be thy name' remind us of both the reality and mystery of God, as Sister Wendy points out:

When we say 'Hallowed be thy name', we're asking that the reality of God be acknowledged. If we're saying this prayer truly, we do acknowledge it. We know he's the great reality but also that mysterious reality. Unless one lives in the freedom and security of that reality, one can miss so much.

She also explains that the Lord's Prayer is both about God *and* about his people, highlighting another reason why God's name should not be taken lightly:

The Our Father is all about God and it's all about us, because God wants his name to be hallowed, for his reality to be understood for our sake, so that we can receive him.

Looking for a father

AN INTERVIEW WITH PAUL COWLEY

'Our Father, who art in heaven'

Paul was brought up in what he now recognizes was a dysfunctional family, with a father he could never really trust and who was often absent. One thing his father did teach his son was 'never to rely on anyone and never to trust anyone because they'll always move away from you'. Unfortunately this lesson was learned all too well. Looking back, Paul realizes that he took this message with him through his school years, his teens, into adulthood and through two failed marriages.

After a career in the army he returned to civilian life and new friendships and challenges. Over dinner one night, he and his girlfriend Amanda discovered that their hosts were Christians and somehow the conversation turned to their faith. Paul remembers, 'I didn't know what Christianity was… and lots of different things ran through my mind about God and his Son, and about my dad, and Clinton [his son from an earlier marriage].' His curiosity led to him attending an Alpha course, on which many of his preconceived ideas about Jesus and the Father God were debunked. But when it came to talking about a 'heavenly father' one could draw near to, Paul felt upset and disturbed. As a child he hadn't been able to draw near to his father and, often left alone, Paul had never received the love and protection he wanted and needed.

The crunch came when he asked himself, 'Why am I frightened of letting God in?' Because of his difficult upbringing Paul found it hard to trust anyone and was scared of making himself vulnerable, and instead had become self-reliant. Nevertheless, somehow he found himself praying: 'If you're up there and all this stuff's true and you want to help me, then let's go for it.' In Paul's words, 'Things started to happen from there', but life wasn't all straightforward.

He was still having problems saying 'Our Father' at the beginning of the Lord's Prayer, a prayer he wanted to say with sincerity. Not only that, but his difficulties with trust and the fatherhood of God were hampering some of the changes he wanted to make in his life as a new Christian. He didn't feel able to marry Amanda because he had already had two failed marriages; he wanted a 'second chance' with his son Clinton and to try to build a relationship with his dysfunctional father. Could he trust God, his heavenly father, not to let him down?

Paul began to pray secretly for things and his faith and trust in God grew as these prayers were answered. He and Amanda now have a 'fantastic' marriage and a daughter named Phoebe; he was able to contact his son Clinton and build a good relationship with him, and he learned to accept and love his father. Paul believes that with God's help he has been given a second chance at fatherhood and at being a 'good dad', for which he's immensely grateful.

For Paul, the relationship with God as father is completely the opposite of what he experienced as a child. He explains how the intimacy that God brings when he loves us as his children has been 'amazingly important' for him to 'grow' as a Christian. He explains, 'I've learned to walk with God and trust him more. I can wander off on my own knowing that he's there, that he trusts me and that when I come back he's always there and will always speak to me.'

When Paul first heard about Jesus using the word 'Abba' or 'Daddy' to address God as his father, he was surprised. But over time he has discovered for himself the personal touch of God, the intimacy that he always longed for from an earthly father and that 'the heavenly father is someone who'll put their arm around me and just hold me'.

'I guess for most of my life I'd been looking for the father I never had as a young boy... Then when I became a Christian I learned that we have a heavenly father who is a good role model and a good father, and my search ended – that's the father I'd been looking for all the time.'

Thy Kingdom come, thy will be done, on earth as it is in heaven

In the Gospels, Jesus often speaks of the kingdom he had come to establish, a kingdom which was very different from the one his followers had in mind and which is far more wonderful than we can imagine today. So what was he asking his followers to pray for? There's a lot to 'unpack' from this phrase.

God's kingdom

As with our ideas of fatherhood, it would be misleading to think of the kingdom of God in earthly terms. It is helpful

40

to read Rowan Williams' views on the nature of this kingdom that we can look forward to:

> *The idea of the kingdom coming was very near the centre of Jesus' teaching. And the kingdom is not a place or a system - it's just a state of affairs when God really is acknowledged to be directing and giving meaning to everything. It's the kingship of God, if you like.*
>
> *So we pray 'God's Kingdom come', meaning let God's will and purpose and God's nature show through in every state of affairs, because that's what it is for God to be king. It's not asking for God to be ordering everyone and everything around but for God in his glory to be visible everywhere. 'Thy Kingdom come' is saying let the world open out to the depth of God's love that is really at the root of it all.*

A kingdom 'in potential'

But if Jesus ushered in the kingdom of God, why do we keep praying 'Thy Kingdom come'? Sister Wendy suggests some answers:

> *... The kingdom, the kingdom of God, the kingdom of heaven: That's what Jesus came to bring. In one sense, he did establish the kingdom - by the incarnation the kingdom has come. It's here already. He is that freedom and joy and love that is the kingdom.*

But, of course, in other ways it hasn't come, not yet, because we're not living in that kingdom visibly. So to pray 'Thy Kingdom come' means we're asking for what Jesus wanted, that his brothers and sisters should love one another. They should live in freedom, they should live as adults, making choices, being responsible, feeding the hungry, clothing the poor, looking after those who are wounded; that's the kingdom. It is here now in potential because Jesus came. He's made it possible for each of us in ourselves to live in that kingdom.

So we pray that we will all learn to become more what Jesus wants us to be, in the kingdom where his will is done on earth as it is in heaven, where we love and care, where we are responsible and, in the best sense, grow up.

As people's lives are transformed by their faith, so it becomes possible to see signs of God's kingdom in the world around us even today. It's both encouraging and challenging to be reminded of this by Rowan Williams:

'The kingdom comes in unexpected ways.'

Jesus himself tells us that the kingdom comes in unexpected ways, it doesn't just come with a great clap of thunder at the end of time, it grows in our midst secretly... It comes through in quirky little moments when people do extraordinary things, take extraordinary risks and

you think, 'Yes, that's a life in which God is showing through...'

Jesus' parables again tell us about people who give up everything because they catch a glimpse of the kingdom, they catch a glimpse of God's beauty. So that's what we're praying for; let the world show God, let God come through.

Doing God's will on earth

In today's world God's will is *not* the first thing that most people do, and even Christians can find it challenging to cooperate with God in what *he* wants. But just as it is possible to see glimpses of God's kingdom here on earth, so there are times when we can experience or observe God's will being done.

So what are we really asking when we pray 'Thy will be done'? What are the implications of this petition? Rowan Williams offers some answers:

We're praying here that the whole universe responds to the gift of God in the same kind of way. 'Thy will be done on earth as it is in heaven.' That tells us, of course, that there's somewhere that God's will is being done and the implication is that it isn't being done very much on earth.

The problem comes with us. Because for us to do God's will is for us to make choices, to make changes. And we're very reluctant to do that, so for us, doing God's will has to be learned; it

'Somewhere...
God's will is
being done.'

doesn't just come automatically for humankind as it seems to for the rest of his creation.

So we ask for help, the help we need to do God's will. We ask for our lives to show God's glory, in the way that the angels singing God's praises, the stars and circling planets are reflecting God's beauty and glory just by being what they are. It's as if there's a huge cosmic choir or orchestra playing God's tune and God's purpose is simply expressed in the order and the beauty of things. So we ask that we may join in that great universal harmony and do God's will in that way. It's not just a matter of doing what God wants moment by moment but, somehow, our lives being in tune with reality.

'Doing God's will has to be learned.'

It's an awesome concept! For anyone who finds it difficult to comprehend what it means for God's will to be done on earth, Sister Wendy suggests that it's really just another way of saying: 'Your will is for us to be free and happy, let it come, let it happen.'

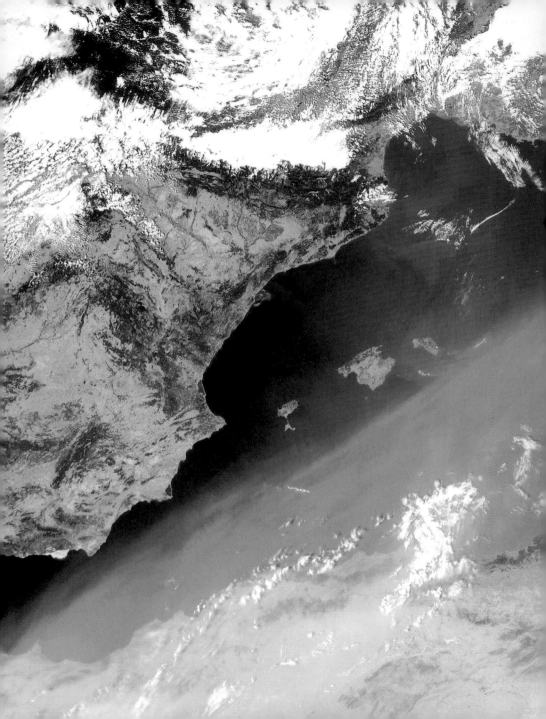

Give us this day our daily bread

At first glance this petition seems straightforward but, as Rowan Williams explains, it's one in which we can find different levels of meaning:

Rivers of ink have been spilt over the exact meaning, but it probably does mean just daily bread, the stuff we need to survive. Yet so much of what Jesus says is shot through with symbolism… and I shouldn't be at all surprised if this was one example.

However, I don't think there's one meaning that we have to settle down with. The simple meaning is: keep us going, give us what we need, all we really need to go on. And yet as soon as we start unpicking that, we ask 'Well, what do we really need?' We don't 'live by bread alone', says Jesus, 'but by every word that comes from God's mouth'. We don't live just by having our material needs fulfilled, we need something more, *and one of the things that we need more of is hope, hope for tomorrow.*

Sister Wendy expands on the nature and significance of 'daily bread':

> *Of course 'bread' here means all you need: all you need physically and all you need spiritually and all you need intellectually, everything, remembering always it won't be the way an earthly father would give it to you.*
>
> *... It won't be bread in a cupboard which you can fall back on when you want, because that's not how grace works. It's the presence of God that he will provide. The presence this day for this day's needs, not necessarily to overcome them but to live through them - because he told us that his greatest joy is that we should have life and have it to the full. What comes this day for each of us can lead us to life or lead us to death. We can grow through it, or we can diminish through it, and praying to God means that we will grow.*

"*Bread*" *here means* all *you need.*'

She continues by explaining why she finds this part of the Lord's Prayer so significant, sharing a visual image that others may find helpful:

> *I think, after the beginning, 'Our Father', the petition I love best is 'Give us this day our daily bread'. It reminds us that God can't give himself to us if we're*

'God can't give himself to us if we're not holding out our hands to him.'

not holding out our hands to him. We have to be aware of what we need, and to be looking at God, to have help. It's there, remember; we only have to ask.

But we won't ask if we're self-sufficient and if we think we can manage. At some level none of us can cope because none of us can say 'I'm living in the kingdom.' No, at best you're longing to live in the kingdom. You're hoping, but you're holding out your hands to make it possible for him to give you that bread that you need, that grace and support, that fulfilment, that life.

Bread for tomorrow

Of course, we cannot ignore the obvious links with the bread consumed at the Eucharist or Communion service, as Rowan Williams points out:

> At least some people in the early church understood this to mean the bread we want for tomorrow or even the bread of tomorrow - give us today tomorrow's bread. Many have

thought that it might mean give us now a taste of the bread we shall eat in the kingdom of God, give us a foretaste of that great banquet and celebration where the universe is drawn together by Christ in the presence of God the Father. And so, for a lot of Christians, that connects with the Holy Communion, of course, because Holy Communion is at one level bread for today; it's very much our daily bread, it's the food we need to keep

going. But it's also a foretaste of the bread of heaven. A foretaste of enjoying the presence of Jesus in heaven at his table at his banquet.

Physical hunger

For many of us it's unlikely that physical hunger is going to be our greatest need, but even for those in need of food, 'daily bread' can have a deeper meaning. Sister Wendy says:

There are so many things that we're lacking in the West. Food isn't the first... but there's understanding, love, kindness, hope perhaps: daily bread. Ask and you'll receive, he tells us, but not in an earthly way. Cling to that in a heavenly way, in the way of the Holy Spirit: he will enable you.

Yet even those in need of food can benefit from other kinds of 'daily bread', as Rowan Williams explains:

It certainly concentrates the mind when you're in an environment where a prayer for daily bread is not just words; but even in such environments you're also made aware that it's not simply bread, it's not just material food, it's hope and dignity that's needed - the sense of being loved and the sense of being welcomed.

Like most of us, Sister Wendy is concerned about those who suffer, but she has observed the remarkable way in which people are sometimes able to draw closer to God in their need.

Some of the poorest people of the world are the ones with the deepest faith. You see, there is no difficulty in saying 'Give us this day our daily bread,' if you understand it's not going to come in a material form; the prayer's for something deeper. Something more fundamental... I don't want to sound glib here, but wouldn't it be better to die of starvation looking trustfully at God, hungry, than to have all the material things you wanted but believing in nothing?

Neither is good. There shouldn't be starvation and when the kingdom does come and we love each other, then there will be no starvation because we rich people will be feeding the poor. So our heavenly father can sometimes give us the gift of the earthly father through what his love has done in us.

And forgive us our trespasses, as we forgive those who trespass against us

Forgiveness is something we all hope to receive from God, and it's certainly something he longs to give, as Sister Wendy reminds us:

> *In the Gospels Jesus speaks about forgiveness… It seems to be a crucial step in coming close to God. Turn to God and say 'I'm sorry' and you know from the parable of the prodigal son what happens: God rushes to you with gifts and joy. That's one of the most beautiful parables in the whole gospel.*

God's forgiveness cannot be earned or deserved, yet this

phrase in the Lord's Prayer reminds us that seeking God's forgiveness for our wrongdoings is directly linked with our willingness to forgive others and the way we treat those who have offended or mistreated us. Sister Wendy points out that it's only our actions that limit God's ability to forgive, as he longs to do:

> It was challenging of Jesus to link together 'forgive us our trespasses, as we forgive those who trespass against us'. I sometimes think people don't quite realize what they're

begging for. You're saying to God, 'Look at the way I treat other people and treat me like that.' It's a very powerful incitement to being loving and forgiving.

What Jesus is saying is that your heart can't turn to God your father for forgiveness if you're not forgiving other people. It makes God's forgiveness impossible. God can't forgive a hard heart. He wants to but he can't, because you can't receive it. Your heart is closed to him. Open your heart to other people and you let him in.

> 'Open your heart to other people and you let God in.'

A bold request

Rowan Williams admits that this part of the Lord's Prayer is one that he finds particularly challenging:

> I think 'forgive us our trespasses' is in some ways one of the most difficult bits of the Lord's Prayer to pray because it reminds us that we're not only saying words, we're expressing a willingness for our lives to be changed. It's a very bold thing to come before God and say 'forgive me because I have forgiven'. And I certainly don't always feel I'm really up to making that kind of claim on God.
>
> It's no good being aware of God's willingness to forgive and saying to him 'forgive me' when we haven't

'It's through God's forgiveness of us that we learn how to forgive.'

begun to understand what it means to forgive... But I think it's saying that it's through God's forgiveness of us that we learn how to forgive. It's in our capacity to forgive that we show we've been forgiven.

He also suggests that the parable of the unforgiving servant provides a powerful reminder of how we can miss out; if you can't forgive, you can't receive forgiveness:

There's Jesus' parable about the servant who's let off his debt and then goes off to somebody indebted to him and crushes that man for his debts; and then the Lord says, 'It's all off, I can't forgive you your debt, you won't forgive others.'

A heavenly role model

We may find forgiving others is difficult, but Rowan Williams believes that there's hope for each one of us as this encouraging analogy shows:

'If you can't forgive, you can't receive forgiveness.'

There's a wonderful image in one of the early church fathers about learning to forgive. He says that it's a bit like teaching a child to do something. The parent does it carefully a few times, then steps back and says, 'Now, you show me.' In the same way God forgives us and then steps back and says, 'Now, you show me how to forgive.'

Forgiving sets you free

AN INTERVIEW WITH BILLY BURNS

'And forgive us our trespasses, as we forgive those who trespass against us.'

Growing up in Northern Ireland in the 1960s, Billy saw the negative effect of lack of forgiveness at first hand, but it wasn't until years later that he had to think about the significance of forgiving others himself. Billy found himself in a situation that was to lead him to a deep and personal understanding of what it means to forgive others and to receive forgiveness. By then he was a practising Christian and saying the Lord's Prayer was part of daily life, but the petition, 'forgive us our trespasses, as we forgive those who trespass against us,' was to assume a far greater importance for Billy.

It all began when Billy was working as a policeman in Bristol. He and a colleague had managed to corner a getaway car after a bank robbery, but then Billy was shot at close range. He was seriously injured, apparently 'very lucky to be alive', and left temporarily paralyzed from the neck down. From the start, Billy harboured no bitterness for Steve, the man who had shot him (something that surprised many people), but he still had to live with the consequences, unable to pretend the horrific incident hadn't happened or to forget it. Years passed and Billy felt that for the most part he had moved on.

Then, ten years later, Steve contacted Billy from Broadmoor to say he was sorry. Billy was initially unsure about Steve's motives but after praying about it he decided to see what Steve had to say. The two men corresponded with one another for some time and it turned out that Steve was quite sincere. Billy realized that 'the guy was serious about repenting... wanting somehow to do something about the damage he'd caused. But when you're in prison for life, what can you do?'

Steve was fortunate because the response he received was all that he'd hoped for. Billy explains why: 'For me to forgive Steve was a natural act; at least, natural if you're a Christian, because of my own forgiveness, the ultimate forgiveness from Christ... We do wrong things and we can't put them right so we require forgiveness from the highest authority, Christ himself. And he gives it to us. So how on earth can we withhold forgiveness from those who have offended us?'

Not only does Billy believe that Christians have

a responsibility to forgive, but also that 'it's an act of wisdom to forgive others because that lack of forgiveness would create bitterness and resentment. It becomes almost cancerous and can have appalling effects on those around and can continue for years.'

'When I say "forgive", I don't mean that I'm condoning or justifying someone else's actions,' he explains. 'I'm simply saying that it is what Christ wants us to do because it lets us set aside hurts and get on with the rest of our lives.' The 'release' that can be experienced by forgiving someone who has hurt or wronged you is something Billy wishes more people could discover for themselves.

Although Steve was not released from prison for another ten years, he and Billy kept in touch and a relationship developed over that time. Since then they have done a number of things together and Billy is able to say, 'My relationship with Steve has enriched my life. It has been very therapeutic, as much to me as it is to him.' And as Steve deals with the consequences of what he did, Billy has found benefits coming out of that — together they hope to be able to discourage others from getting into crime.

The men's ongoing relationship is one that fascinates other people and one that Billy might once have thought impossible. He is quick to tell others that it has come about only 'because as a Christian I am able to forgive Steve and respond to his desire to make peace with me... It just shows what can happen when God's in things and when you take on Christ's advice in the Lord's Prayer to forgive others as God forgives us.'

Lead us not into temptation, but deliver us from evil

It has been said that this is one of the hardest parts of the Lord's Prayer to understand. This may be true, but these words can also be an encouragement, reminding us that God is with us in the difficult times that we may all face. Although the two parts of this petition are inextricably linked, it's helpful to begin by looking at them separately.

A strange request

'Lead us not into temptation,' seems rather a strange thing to ask God as Sister Wendy observes:

'Lead us not into temptation' is an enigmatic phrase. Obviously the last thing God will do is to lead us into temptation. But Jesus knew so well, from his own experiences in the wilderness after his baptism, that temptation is part of being human. Each one of us is going to be tempted.

So what are we to make of this? Sister Wendy continues by sharing her understanding of the original Hebrew phraseology and how this might clarify what we are asking for:

He's saying 'Be with us in temptation', not 'Take it away', because you can't be human and not have temptation. I believe Jesus means, 'Help me with temptation.'

So when temptation comes - as come it will - we ask 'Be with me, deliver me from the evil of temptation, keep me safe' - and he will. He'll help you cope with it. So a more contemporary expression would be, 'Help me to cope with temptation.'

Temptation is something people tend to think is wrong, and that if we loved God we wouldn't be tempted. Jesus has shown us it is not. The way some people act may make you furiously angry, that's human. Showing it, acting on it, being angry back, that's not the action of somebody who loves God.

'A more contemporary expression would be, "Help me to cope with temptation."'

Rowan Williams believes that, seen in the context of Jesus' own day, the word 'temptation' means much more than, for example, an impulse to do unworthy or sinful things:

Jesus' teaching often returns to this idea that a great time of trial or crisis is coming. A time when we shall find out what we're really capable of. So it's worthwhile praying to God, 'Give us what we need to face crisis when it comes and please God don't let us be precipitated into that too soon...' Pray that when the time of trial comes, when things get really difficult, you will have the resources to meet it.

Set us free

For both Rowan Williams and Sister Wendy the phrase
'But deliver us from evil' is a natural progression from

'Lead us not into temptation'. Sister Wendy reflects on the nature of evil:

> *The evil of falling into temptation, that is the only evil. There is no other real evil except that of sinning. There are other things, dreadful, painful things, to be avoided at all costs if we can, but they're not evil. Evil is sin. Blotting God out, hurting others or his world. The temptation to put yourself first and use other people is constant, it's with us all the time. But using other people to their detriment is sin, is evil. And we ask to be helped to cope with that constant temptation.*

Continuing with the idea of being ready to face an impending crisis, Rowan Williams shows how 'Deliver us from evil' might also be interpreted as 'Set us free':

> *'Deliver us from evil': set us free. Set us free from all those things, the fears, the sins, the selfish habits that keep us prisoner and that make us unable to face a crisis... Because the time of crisis is when the devil, the enemy of humanity, is really making hay. He's having a wonderful time because when there's lots of fear and uncertainty, then the devil can come in and manipulate us and reinforce all that's most inhuman in us. And whether or not people these days believe in a personal devil, I think the idea of the principle or the power of*

evil coming in to make the most of our weakness and our fear still makes sense. So we can still quite rightly pray to be delivered - set free - from that.

For thine is the kingdom, the power and the glory, for ever and ever. Amen.

This short closing phrase, found in the traditional version of the Lord's Prayer, is generally accepted not to have been part of the prayer Jesus shared with his followers, yet it seems to contain the essence of what the prayer is all about. Not only does it remind us of the person to whom the prayer is addressed but it is also a verse of praise and thanksgiving in anticipation of the earlier petitions being answered by a powerful and glorious God. It is fitting that the Lord's Prayer ends with the word 'Amen' or 'so be it', uniting the family of believers who share in saying its words.

Closing thoughts: significance in simplicity

The Lord's Prayer is not an easy prayer... It's a prayer that requires our lives to change, that we become different sorts of people... and that will only happen when we learn how to depend freely and lovingly on the God who's made himself Our Father.
ROWAN WILLIAMS

The Our Father is a wonderful expression, I believe, of the creed taken down to its very fundamentals.
SISTER WENDY

If somebody said, 'Give me a summary of Christian faith on the back of an envelope', the best thing to do would be to write the Lord's Prayer.
ROWAN WILLIAMS

The Our Father sums up the whole message of Jesus. It's Christianity in miniature. If somebody were to say to me, 'Tell me what Christianity's about', I'd go through the whole of the Our Father, and there would be nothing that one would need to add.
SISTER WENDY

Picture Acknowledgments

Endpapers: Michael Melford/Getty Images

Title page: Warren Marr/Panoramic Images/NGSImages.com

p. 9: Royalty-Free/Corbis

pp. 12–13: Hitoshi Nishimura/Getty Images

p. 16: Digital Vision

p. 22: Royalty-Free/Corbis

p. 25: Imagestopshop/Alamy

p. 26: Royalty-Free/Corbis

p. 29: 2006 Punchstock

p. 30: Royalty-Free/Corbis

pp. 32–33: Pete Turner/Getty Images Ltd

p. 43: Digital Vision

pp. 46–47: NASA, Modis Rapid Response Team at GSFC

p. 49: Hein Von Horsten/Getty Images Ltd

p. 50: Stock Connection Distribution/Alamy

p. 53: Alain Couillaud/Alamy

p. 54: Blickwinkel/Alamy

p. 58: Neal and Molly Jansen/Alamy

p. 60: Jodi Cobb/National Geographic Image Collection

pp. 68–69: Jonathan Self

p. 72: Digital Vision

Endpapers: Andrea Pistolesi/Getty Images Ltd